ALLERGY AVE.

WE JUST WANNA EAT!

By Domo Jones

ALLERGY CHRONICLES

Hey, I'm Domo, and let me tell you, living with food allergies is like navigating a minefield – one wrong move, and boom, you're down for the count. But here's the thing: I've learned a lot on this journey, and I figured it's time to share the knowledge I've picked up along the way.

I've always had to be cautious about what I eat. You know, the usual: dairy, peanuts, the basic stuff you learn to avoid growing up. I was pretty good at dodging the usual suspects. But life has a way of throwing you curveballs when you least expect it. One day, I found myself facing off against seafood, and trust me, it won that round.

ALLERGY CHRONICLES

It was a normal day—nothing out of the ordinary—until suddenly, I couldn't breathe. My throat closed up, my skin flared, and next thing I knew, I was in anaphylactic shock. Not exactly a fun way to spend your afternoon, right? That moment changed everything for me. The next two weeks? Absolute chaos. It was Benadryl city: two, sometimes three times a day. My meals? Beef jerky, rice cakes, and water. That's it. I was basically a survivalist in my own kitchen.

During that time, I realized how important it is to know what you're up against. How easy it is for something small, like cross-contamination, to send you to the ER. And it's not just about food. It's about everything around food—how it's prepared, what it touches, even who's handling it. I became a detective, figuring out the tiniest details that could cause a reaction.

ALLERGY CHRONICLES

That's when I decided: why not share what I've learned? There are tons of people like me, walking through life avoiding their allergens like ninjas, and then there are others who have no idea what it's like. Whether you have allergies yourself or you're just around someone who does, I want to help. If you can avoid spending time in the hospital, that's a win.

So here's the deal: this book is going to be part guide, part story, and hopefully, a lot of fun. I'm going to share everything—tips for avoiding allergic reactions, how to navigate food labels like a pro, how to handle cross-contamination in the kitchen, and even how to create a solid emergency plan. It's going to be real, it's going to be useful, and most importantly, it's going to keep you out of trouble.

Because, at the end of the day, we just want to eat. And we deserve to eat safely. So let's dive in and figure this thing out together!

Understanding allergy symptoms

Symptoms can be subtle and go unnoticed.

Some common symptoms

(Swipe)

Allergy: Dairy

Symptoms: Stomach cramps, vomiting, hives, diarrhea, anaphylaxis.

Examples:
Milk
cheese
yogurt
butter

ALLERGY:

Peanut

Symptoms: Hives, swelling (especially of the face, lips, and throat), difficulty breathing, anaphylaxis.

EXAMPLES:

Peanut Butter
Peanut oil
Mixed nuts
containing peanuts

ALLERGY:
Eggs

Symptoms: Skin rashes, hives, nasal congestion, stomach pain, anaphylaxis

EXAMPLES:
Scrambled eggs
Baked goods containing eggs
Mayonnaise

Allergy: Wheat

Symptoms: Skin irritation, hives, nasal congestion, digestive issues, anaphylaxis.

Examples:

- Bread
- Pasta
- Cereal
- Baked Goods

Allergy:

Shellfish

Symptoms: Hives, swelling, wheezing, difficulty breathing, anaphylaxis

Examples:
Shrimp
Crab
Oysters
Clams
Crab

ALLERGY AVE.

WE JUST WANNA EAT!

UNDERSTANDING FOOD ALLERGIES

A lot of people mix up food allergies with food intolerents

HERE'S THE DIFFERENCE:
(Swipe)

Food Allergy:
Peanut Allergy

Description: A peanut allergy is an immune system response to peanut proteins, where the body mistakenly identifies them as harmful.

Symptoms:

Mild Symptoms:
- Hives or rash
- Itching or tingling in the mouth or throat
- Swelling of the lips, face, tongue, or throat

Severe Symptoms (Anaphylaxis):
- Difficulty breathing
- Swelling of the throat that can block airflow
- Rapid drop in blood pressure
- Dizziness or fainting
- Rapid pulse
- Loss of consciousness

Food intolerant:

Lactose Intolerance

Description: Lactose intolerance occurs when the body lacks enough lactase, an enzyme needed to digest lactose, a sugar found in milk and dairy products.

Symptoms:

- Bloating
- Gas
- Diarrhea
- Stomach cramps or pain
- Nausea

Key Differences:

- Cause: A food allergy involves the immune system, while food intolerance involves the digestive system.
- Severity: Food allergies can be severe and life-threatening, requiring immediate treatment. Food intolerances typically cause discomfort but are not life-threatening.
- Onset: Allergic reactions can occur within minutes of consuming the allergen. Intolerance symptoms often develop more slowly, usually within a few hours.

ALLERGY AVE.

WE JUST WANNA EAT!

Read Food Labels

Often times there could be hidden allergens in food products that you're not aware of

WHAT TO WATCH OUT FOR:

(Swipe)

WHY IT MATTERS:
Natural & Artificial Flavors

These terms can sometimes hide allergens.

TIP:

If the label includes "natural flavors" or "artificial flavors" without specifying ingredients, contact the manufacturer for clarification.

Why it matters:

Allergen Warning Section

Many packaged foods must list the top eight allergens (milk, eggs, fish, shellfish, tree nuts, peanuts, wheat, and soybeans) if they are present.

Tip:

Look for phrases like "Contains [allergen]" near the ingredients list. Also, check for "May contain" or "Processed in a facility with [allergen]," as cross-contamination can occur.

Gluten-Free or Allergy Free Labels

Foods labeled as "gluten-free" must meet FDA requirements, but always check the ingredient list in case of contamination or other allergens.

TIP:

Products that are labeled "free from [allergen]" or "gluten-free" must meet specific standards. However, cross-contamination may still be possible, so be cautious.

Why it matters:

Food Additives & Pressrvatives

Some preservatives or additives can be derived from allergens, particularly soy, wheat, or milk.

Tip:

Look for terms like "hydrolyzed vegetable protein" (often derived from soy or wheat) and "modified food starch" (which may contain wheat).

Why it matters:

"Free Form" Claims

Labels like "dairy-free" or "nut-free" don't guarantee the product is free from cross-contamination.

Tip:

Ensure that the product is made in an allergen-free facility or contact the company for more details

Total fat

Too much saturated fat can raise bad cholesterol levels, increasing heart disease risk. Trans fats are even worse and should be avoided entirely.

Look for low levels of saturated fat (less than 5g per serving) and avoid trans fats.

Hidden Names of Allergens

- <u>Milk</u>: Look for casein, whey, lactalbumin, or lactose.
- <u>Eggs</u>: Watch for albumin, globulin, and words containing "oval-" (e.g., ovalbumin).
- <u>Fish/Shellfish</u>: Different species of fish or shellfish may not be clearly listed. Watch for terms like "surimi" (imitation crab) and specific types like shrimp, cod, or anchovies.
- <u>Peanuts</u>: Peanut oil, groundnut, or Arachis oil are other names for peanuts.
- <u>Tree Nuts</u>: Look for specific nuts like almonds, walnuts, or cashews. Also, nut derivatives such as nut butter and oils.
- <u>Soy</u>: Soy lecithin, hydrolyzed soy protein, or soy sauce can be hidden sources.
- <u>Wheat</u>: Look for terms like gluten, durum, farina, semolina, and spelt.

TIP:

Allergens may be listed under unfamiliar names. Here's what to look for.

Cross contamination

Cross-contamination in others and Restaurant kitchens can trigger reactions.

Steps to avoid a reaction

(Swipe)

Hand Hygiene

TIP:
Wash hands with soap and water before and after handling different foods, especially allergens.

TIP:
Avoid hand sanitizers for allergens; they may not remove all traces of allergens.

Separate Utensils and Cookware

Tip:

Use color-coded utensils or labels to distinguish between regular and allergen-safe tools.

Tip:

Use separate cutting boards, knives, and utensils for allergenic foods.

(CONT...)

Separate Utensils and Cookware

TIP:

Do not use the same toaster, blender, or mixer for allergen-free and allergen-containing food unless thoroughly cleaned.

TIP:

Have dedicated pots, pans, and serving utensils for allergen-free meals.

Thorough Cleaning of Surfaces and Utensils

TIP:
Clean countertops, tables, and cooking surfaces with soap and water before and after preparing food.

TIP:
Use disposable paper towels instead of dishcloths to clean surfaces, as cloth towels can spread allergens.

TIP:
Wash utensils, plates, and cutting boards in hot, soapy water or in a dishwasher after each use.

Labeling and Organization

TIP:

Clearly label containers, drawers, and cabinets fo
allergen-safe items.

TIP:

Keep pre-packaged allergen-safe foods sealed
and separate from foods that contain allergens

TIP:

If using bulk bins (e.g., for flour or grains), have
dedicated scoops for each container.

Washing Your Hands After Eating

TIP:

After consuming allergen-containing foods, wash hands, and brush teeth to avoid spreading allergens, especially when interacting with someone with a severe allergy.

Educate Everyone in the Household

TIP:

Make sure everyone in the household knows about the importance of these steps and practices them consistently.

Careful Use of Appliances

TIP:
Clean microwaves, ovens, and stovetops between uses, especially if cooking allergen-containing foods.

TIP:
Shared grills or toasters unless thoroughly cleaned or lined with foil.

Storage Tips

TIP:
Keep allergen-free foods on higher shelves to avoid accidental spills or contamination from other items.

TIP:
Store allergen-containing foods in sealed containers or separate shelves.

TIP:
Use separate storage containers for allergen-safe foods to avoid cross-contact.

Use of Disposable Items

For especially sensitive allergies, consider
using disposable plates, cups, and cutlery to
further reduce risk.

If hosting others, serve allergen-free
foods with separate serving spoons and
plates to prevent guests from mixing
foods.

ALLERGY AVE.

WE JUST WANNA EAT!

Safe Cooking Practices

Cooking at home can still be risky.

Ways to stay safe:

(Swipe)

Serve Allergen-Free Food First

TIP:

Serve allergen-free foods before allergenic dishes to ensure there's no contamination through shared utensils or plates.

TIP:

Avoid double-dipping: Use separate serving utensils for each dish and avoid dipping allergen-containing utensils into allergen-free dishes.

Avoid Shared Appliances

Tip:

Don't use toasters, grills, or deep fryers tha[t] have been in contact with allergens unless they've been thoroughly cleaned.

Tip:

Use separate blenders and mixers for allerge[n] free ingredients, or clean them thoroughly between uses.

Don't Reuse Marinades or Sauces

TIP:

Avoid using marinades, sauces, or oils that have come into contact with allergenic foods for allergen-free dishes.

TIP:

Have separate serving spoons and containers for allergen-free sauces or condiments.

Label Allergen-Free Foods Clearly

TIP:
Use labels or separate containers for allergen-free foods, especially when storing leftovers.

TIP:
In group settings, clearly mark allergen-safe dishes so there's no confusion during serving.

Use Foil or Parchment Paper for Baking

TIP:
Line baking trays and pans with foil or parchment paper when cooking allergen-free meals to prevent direct contact with surfaces that may have had allergens on them.

TIP:
If using a grill, place foil down on the grill to prevent cross-contact between allergenic and allergen-free items.

Cook Allergen-Free Foods First

If cooking both allergenic and allergen-free foods, keep allergen-free items covered until they're served to prevent airborne cross-contact (e.g., flour or oil splatters).

Prepare allergen-free foods first to reduce the risk of contamination from cooking equipment or surfaces.

Use Separate Utensils and Cookware

TIP:
Have dedicated knives, spatulas, pots, and pans for allergen-free foods, or thoroughly clean utensils before switching between allergenic and non-allergenic foods.

TIP:
Use separate cutting boards for allergenic and allergen-free ingredients to avoid cross-contact.

Clean as You Go

TIP:
Wipe down surfaces like countertops, stovetops, and tables with hot soapy water or disinfectant wipes frequently during food prep, especially if allergens were involved.

TIP:
Clean appliances like mixers, blenders, and food processors thoroughly if they've been used for allergens before preparing allergen-free meals.

TIP:
Use disposable paper towels for cleaning allergen-containing spills instead of reusable cloths.

Use Dedicated Allergen-Free Zones

TIP:
Designate specific areas of your kitchen for preparing allergen-free meals. For example, one side of the counter can be used exclusively for allergen-free food prep.

TIP:
Create a safe prep station with separate cutting boards, utensils, and appliances like blenders or toasters for allergen-free cooking.

TIP:
Keep allergen-free and allergen-containing foods separate to avoid accidental mixing.

Wash Hands Frequently

TIP:
After touching allergens: Always wash hands after handling foods containing allergens to prevent accidental cross-contact.

TIP:
Before cooking: Wash hands with soap and water for at least 20 seconds before handling any food.

TIP:
Before serving food: Wash hands again before serving allergen-free foods to avoid any contamination.

ALLERGY AVE.

WE JUST WANNA EAT!

Dining Out with Allergies

Eating out can be a minefield when you're unsure of every ingredient on the menu.

Ways to stay ready:

(Swipe)

Choose Allergy-Friendly Restaurants

TIP:

Research Ahead: Look for restaurants that are known for accommodating allergies or have allergen-friendly menus. Online reviews and allergen-specific apps can help identify safe options.

TIP:

Chain Restaurants: Many chain restaurants have detailed allergen information and standardized processes, making it easier to find safe meals.

Communicate Clearly with Staff

TIP:

<u>Inform Your Server Immediately:</u> As soon as you're seated, let your server know about any allergies. Be clear and specific about what you cannot eat and the severity of your allergy.

TIP:

<u>Ask Questions:</u> Don't hesitate to ask how dishes are prepared, whether cross-contamination is a risk, and whether substitutions can be made.

TIP:

<u>Speak to a Manager or Chef:</u> For complex allergies, ask to speak with a manager or chef to ensure that your needs are communicated effectively to the kitchen staff.

Read the Menu Carefully

TIP:

<u>Look for Allergy Indicators</u>: Some menus clearly indicate allergens like nuts, dairy, or gluten. Always double-check with the staff even if something seems safe.

TIP:

<u>Avoid Buffets</u>: Buffets can pose a high risk of cross-contamination due to shared utensils and proximity of different foods.

Be Aware of Cross-Contamination

TIP:
Ask About Prep Areas: Ensure that the restaurant has protocols to avoid cross-contamination, such as separate fryers for gluten-free food or dedicated prep stations for allergen-free meals.

TIP:
Inquire About Cooking Methods: If a dish is grilled, fried, or sautéed, ask if it's cooked on shared surfaces or with shared oils.

Bring a Chef's Card

TIP:

Prewritten Allergen Information: Carry a small card listing your allergies and any cooking instructions. Handing this to your server or the chef can help avoid misunderstandings, especially in busy restaurants.

Go During Off-Peak Hours

TIP:

Less Crowded, More Attention: Dining when the restaurant is less busy means staff can give more attention to your dietary needs and may reduce the risk of mistakes.

ALLERGY AVE.

WE JUST WANNA EAT!

Emergency Action Plan

Not knowing what to do during an allergic reaction can add more problems to calming your allergic reaction

Ways to stay prepared:

(Swipe)

Recognize the Symptoms of an Allergic Reaction

- Mild Symptoms: Itching, hives, sneezing, swelling of the lips or face, mild stomach discomfort.

- Severe Symptoms (Anaphylaxis): Difficulty breathing, wheezing, swelling of the throat, chest tightness, dizziness or fainting, rapid heartbeat, severe hives, or a drop in blood pressure.

Administer Epinephrine (EpiPen or Similar Auto-Injector)

Step 1: Remove the Auto-Injector from Its Case

Grasp the auto-injector firmly and remove the safety cap (usually blue or orange, depending on the brand).

Step 2: Position the Auto-Injector

- Hold the injector in your dominant hand with the needle end pointing down.

Press the injector firmly into the middle of the outer thigh (through clothing if necessary).

((CONT...)

Administer Epinephrine (EpiPen or Similar Auto-Injector)

STEP 3: ADMINISTER THE INJECTION

- Push down firmly until you hear or feel a click, signaling that the epinephrine has been injected.
- Hold the auto-injector in place for 3-5 seconds to ensure the full dose is delivered.

STEP 4: REMOVE THE INJECTOR

- After 3-5 seconds, remove the injector and massage the injection site for about 10 seconds to help the epinephrine absorb.
- Be aware that the injection site may be sore or bruised afterward.

Call 911 or Emergency Services Immediately

- **After Using the EpiPen, Dial 911:** Even if symptoms improve, anaphylaxis can return, so emergency medical attention is necessary.

- **Inform the Dispatcher of the Situation:** Let them know you used an epinephrine auto-injector and describe the allergic reaction symptoms.

Monitor the Person Closely

- **Watch for Recurrence of Symptoms:** Sometimes symptoms can return (biphasic reaction), so continue to monitor breathing and alertness.

- **Administer a Second Dose if Necessary:** If symptoms persist or return and help hasn't arrived within 5-15 minutes, use a second auto-injector if available.

Stay Calm and Reassure the Person

- Keep the Person Comfortable: Encourage them to stay still, lying flat with their feet elevated unless they're having trouble breathing.

- Remain with the Person: Stay close until emergency medical personnel arrive and provide any relevant medical history to the paramedics.

Follow-Up with a Doctor

- Hospital Evaluation: After the emergency, a doctor will need to evaluate the patient, as anaphylaxis can have ongoing effects or require further treatment.

- Renew Your Auto-Injector Prescription: If an auto-injector was used, ensure you get a replacement and follow up with an allergist to adjust your action plan if needed.

Additional Tips:

- **Always Carry Two Epinephrine Auto-Injectors:** In case a second dose is needed.

- **Wear a Medical Alert Bracelet:** This helps others quickly identify your allergies in an emergency.

ALLERGY AVE.

WE JUST WANNA EAT!

ood Allergy Testing

It's safe to always stay abreast of new or unknown food allergies you may not know you have

Ways to stay alert:

(Swipe)

Skin Prick Test (SPT)

- **What It Is:** A small amount of suspected allergens is placed on the skin, usually on the forearm or back, and the skin is pricked with a needle. If you are allergic to a substance, a small raised bump (like a mosquito bite) will appear at the test site within 15-20 minutes.

- **What It Tests For:** Pollen, dust mites, mold, pet dander, and certain foods.

- **When to Consider:** If you have symptoms such as frequent sneezing, runny nose, itchy eyes, skin rashes, or digestive issues after eating certain foods.

Intradermal Skin Test

- **What It Is:** Similar to the skin prick test, but instead of placing allergens on the surface of the skin, a small amount of allergen is injected just below the skin's surface.

- **What It Tests For:** Often used for insect venom or when a skin prick test does not yield clear results.

- **When to Consider:** If a skin prick test comes back negative, but allergy symptoms persist, especially for allergens like insect stings or penicillin.

Patch Test

• **What It Is:** Small patches containing allergens are applied to the skin, usually on the back, and left for 48 hours. The healthcare provider checks for reactions over several days.

• **What It Tests For:** Contact allergens such as metals (like nickel), fragrances, and latex, which cause delayed reactions (contact dermatitis).

• **When to Consider:** If you experience skin reactions (e.g., redness, blistering, or itching) after exposure to certain products like cosmetics, jewelry, or cleaning agents.

Blood Test (Specific IgE Test)

- **What It Is:** A blood sample is drawn and analyzed for specific antibodies (IgE) that the immune system produces in response to allergens.

- **What It Tests For:** Can detect a wide range of allergens, including pollen, foods, pet dander, and more.

- **When to Consider:** If you have a skin condition like eczema that may interfere with skin testing, or if you're taking medications that could affect skin test results (like antihistamines).

Oral Food Challenge

- **What It Is:** In a controlled medical setting, you consume increasing amounts of a suspected allergenic food while being monitored for reactions.

- **What It Tests For:** Food allergies, especially when other tests (like blood or skin tests) are inconclusive.

- **When to Consider:** If you suspect a food allergy and need a definitive diagnosis, or if you're testing to see if a food allergy has been outgrown.

Elimination Diet

- What It Is: Certain foods are removed from your diet for several weeks, and then reintroduced one at a time to monitor for allergic reactions.

- What It Tests For: Food sensitivities or intolerances, such as reactions to dairy, gluten, or other common allergens.

- When to Consider: If you experience digestive issues, fatigue, or skin problems that seem to be related to your diet but are difficult to pinpoint.

When to Consider Allergy Testing

- Frequent respiratory issues like sneezing, coughing, or wheezing.

- Persistent skin conditions, such as rashes or eczema, especially after exposure to certain products.

- Digestive problems like bloating or nausea after eating specific foods.

- Recurrent reactions to insect stings or certain medications.

- Chronic sinus infections or asthma that could be triggered by environmental factors.

Follow-Up with a Doctor

- Hospital Evaluation: After the emergency, a doctor will need to evaluate the patient, as anaphylaxis can have ongoing effects or require further treatment.

- Renew Your Auto-Injector Prescription: If an auto-injector was used, ensure you get a replacement and follow up with an allergist to adjust your action plan if needed.

ALLERGY AVE.

WE JUST WANNA EAT!

Traveling with Food Allergies

Stick to eating foods that you're certain you are not allergic to. It prevents unwaranted reactions while away

Ways to stay prepared:

(Swipe)

Packing List for Traveling with Food Allergies

1. Nut-Free Granola Bars (verify if nut-free is needed)

2. Gluten-Free Crackers or Rice Cakes

3. Fruit Packs or Dried Fruit

4. Individual Peanut Butter or Sunflower Seed Butter Packets (if safe for your allergies)

5. Jerky or Meat Snacks (from trusted brands)

Packing List for Traveling with Food Allergies

6. Allergen-Free Trail Mix (e.g., seed-based instead of nut-based)

7. Popcorn or Pretzels (check for allergen labels)

8. Gluten-Free or Dairy-Free Cookies

9. Allergen-Free Chocolate or Protein Bars (confirm they're free of your allergens)

10. Instant Oatmeal Cups (just add hot water)

Learn Key Allergy Phrases

- "I have a food allergy to [allergen]."

- "Can you tell me what ingredients are in this?"

- "Does this contain [allergen]?"

- "Is this dish safe for someone with [allergen]?"

- "Please prepare this meal without [allergen]."

Research Allergy-Friendly Restaurants

- **Find Allergy-Aware Restaurants:** Use apps like AllergyEats, Spokin, or TripAdvisor to find restaurants that cater to food allergies.

- **Call Ahead:** If possible, call the restaurant in advance to confirm their ability to accommodate your allergies.

ALLERGY AVE.

WE JUST WANNA EAT!

EDUCATING FRIENDS & FAMILY

It's always safe to let the people you're commonly around understand and know the different allergies and affects you have from certain foods.

WAYS TO STAY PREPARED:

(Swipe)

Explain the Severity

- Be Clear About the Risk: Start by explaining that food allergies can range from mild reactions to life-threatening anaphylaxis. Make sure they understand the seriousness of even small amounts of allergens.

- Describe Your Allergies: Be specific about what you are allergic to (e.g., nuts, dairy, gluten) and how exposure can affect you. Share personal stories or examples to illustrate your experiences.

Outline the Symptoms to Watch For

- **List Common Symptoms:** Help them recognize signs of an allergic reaction, including hives, swelling, difficulty breathing, and dizziness.

- **Emphasize Severe Reactions:** Make sure they understand the symptoms of anaphylaxis (throat tightening, wheezing, drop in blood pressure) and that immediate action is needed

Teach Them How to Use an Epinephrine Auto-Injector

- Show Them How to Administer It: Give a quick demonstration of how to use your epinephrine auto-injector (EpiPen or similar), explaining when and how to use it if you have a severe reaction.

- Practice with a Trainer Pen: If they're open to it, let them practice using a trainer injector so they feel more confident about handling an emergency.

Explain the Importance of Avoiding Cross-Contamination

- **Discuss Cross-Contact Risks:** Teach them how even trace amounts of allergens from shared surfaces, utensils, or cooking oil can cause a reaction.

- **Offer Solutions:** Suggest using separate utensils, cutting boards, and pans when preparing food, and encourage thorough cleaning between uses to avoid contamination

Suggest Ways They Can Help with Food Preparation

- **Invite Them to Help You Cook:** This is a good way for them to see firsthand how to prepare food safely. You can guide them on reading labels, checking for hidden allergens, and avoiding risky ingredients.

- **Offer Recipe Substitutes:** Provide alternatives for common allergens in recipes (e.g., dairy-free milk, gluten-free flour) so they can make meals you can enjoy.

ALLERGY AVE.

WE JUST WANNA EAT!

Workplace Safety

Having a precaution of understanding that the working environment is a commune space, will help prevent a lot of cross-contamination.

Keep Allergy-Safe Snacks

TIP:

eep a stock of allergen-free snacks at your desk, especially if your office has communal snacks that may contain allergens.

TIP:

If you're organizing office snacks, choose allergen-friendly options or clearly label those that contain allergens.

Have an Emergency Plan in Place

TIP:
Carry your epinephrine auto-injector (EpiPen) wit
you at all times if you have severe allergies, and
make sure it's easily accessible.

TIP:

Have an emergency contact list: Make sure
coworkers know who to contact (911, your
emergency contact, etc.) if you have a reaction

(CONT...)

Have an Emergency Plan in Place

TIP:

Coworkers on how to respond in case of an allergic reaction. Teach them how to use your epinephrine auto-injector and what symptoms to watch for.

TIP:

Keep a medical alert card or bracelet with details about your allergies in case of an emergency.

Educate Your Colleagues

TIP:
Share educational resources or have a short meeting to explain the seriousness of food allergies and how to prevent cross-contact.

TIP:
Encourage coworkers to ask questions and learn about reading food labels to help create a more allergy-aware environment.

Use Cleaning Practices

TIP:
Clean shared surfaces like breakroom tables, desks, and chairs with disinfecting wipes if allergens are present.

TIP:
Encourage a clean-desk policy, particularly after meals, to minimize the risk of allergen exposure.

Advocate for a Supportive Workplace

TIP:

Suggest policies or guidelines for food allergy management, such as avoiding certain allergens in the office or requesting regular cleaning of shared spaces.

TIP:

Advocate for access to first-aid kits that include allergy medications like antihistamines and auto-injectors.

Communicate Clearly About Your Allergies

TIP:

Inform your colleagues and manager about your food allergies so they can be mindful when sharing food or organizing office events.

TIP:

Label your food in the shared refrigerator with clear "allergen-free" notes to prevent others from accidentally contaminating it.

TIP:

Post reminders in shared kitchen areas, like "Please avoid bringing peanuts into the office" if you have severe allergies.

Lunchtime Etiquette

TIP:

Avoid sharing food: Politely ask colleagues not to share food, as cross-contamination could occur if their food contains allergens.

TIP:

Be cautious about office potlucks or catered events. Bring your own allergen-free food, or ask the organizer to accommodate your allergies.

TIP:

Encourage labeling food at office events: If food is brought in for the office, ask that ingredients or allergens be clearly labeled

Create a Safe Eating Environment

TIP:

Designate an allergen-free area in the lunchroom where those with food allergies can eat safely.

TIP:

Encourage employees to wash their hands and clean surfaces after eating allergenic foods, especially in common areas

TIP:

you have a severe allergy, you may want to eat at separate table or eat meals at your desk to minimize exposure risks.

Avoid Cross-Contamination in Shared Kitchens

TIP:
Clean shared appliances like microwaves or toasters thoroughly before use, or bring your own to avoid cross contact.

TIP:
Use separate kitchen tools like cutting boards, utensils, and microwaves for allergen-free food preparation.

TIP:
Store your food in sealed containers in the office fridge to prevent accidental contamination from other foods

Be Prepared During Office Events and Travel

TIP:

When dining out with colleagues, choose restaurants that offer allergen-friendly options and clearly communicate your allergies to the staff.

TIP:

Bring your own allergy-safe snacks or meals to work-related events when necessary.

TIP:

Bring your own allergy-safe snacks or meals to work-related events when necessary.

Now, Let's Eat!

So here we are, at the end of this journey. If there's one thing I hope you take away from all this, it's that living with food allergies doesn't have to feel like walking on eggshells. Yes, it can be overwhelming at times, and sure, it takes a little extra effort—but trust me, it's manageable. We can still enjoy good food, good company, and good times, as long as we're prepared.

Whether you're someone dealing with severe food allergies yourself or someone who cares about someone with them, you now have the tools to navigate this world more confidently. From understanding labels, managing cross-contamination, and creating allergen-free zones, to having an emergency plan in place —these are just a few ways to take control and make life with food allergies safer and easier.

Now, let's eat!

Remember, we don't want anything fancy or complicated. At the end of the day, we just want to eat. Safely. Happily. And without worry.

Thank you for joining me on this journey. Stay safe, stay informed, and enjoy the foods that fuel you—because life's too short to live in fear of what's on your plate.

Love you, domo!

Nutrition Facts

Serving Size:

% Daily Value*

Food allergies are no joke—but managing them doesn't have to be impossible. Whether you're living with severe allergies or supporting someone who does, this book is your ultimate guide to navigating a world full of hidden risks while still enjoying life to the fullest.

Join Domo as she shares her personal journey of surviving anaphylactic shock, mastering food labels, avoiding cross-contamination, and creating safe spaces to eat and live. Packed with practical tips, real-life stories, and actionable advice, this book is designed to educate and empower.

From understanding the dangers of hidden allergens to creating allergen-free zones at work, home, and on the go, We Just Want to Eat equips readers with the tools they need to thrive safely.

Because at the end of the day, it's simple: we just want to eat—without fear, without worry, and with plenty of joy.

100%
ORGANIC

www.ingramcontent.com/pod-product-compliance
Lightning Source LLC
Chambersburg PA
CBHW050754160726
48004CB00002B/552